Peter Lamborn Wilson

Angels

Messengers of the Gods

with 87 illustrations 16 in color

Thames and Hudson

ART AND IMAGINATION

© 1980 and 1994 Thames and Hudson Ltd, London

First published in Great Britain in 1980
This abridged edition first published in paperback in the
United States of America in 1994 by
Thames and Hudson Inc., 500 Fifth Avenue,
New York, New York 10110

Library of Congress Catalog Card Number 93-61374

ISBN 0-500-81044-3

Printed and bound in Singapore

Contents

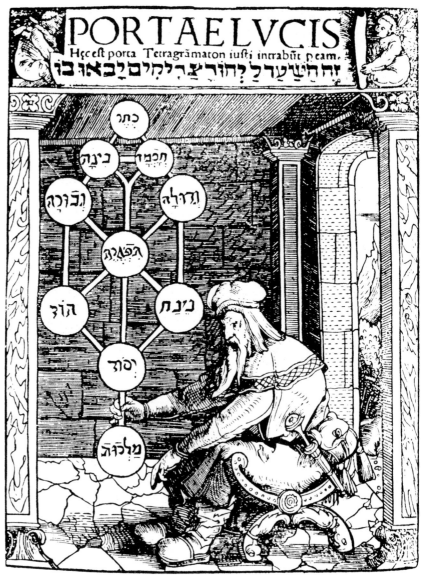

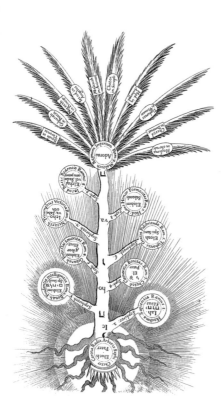

Two diagrams of the Sefirothic Tree, showing the Divine Attributes, the Jewish mystical system enshrined in the Kabbalah. *Above:* from Robert Fludd's *Philosophia Sacra*, 1626. *Right:* from Paulus Ricius' *Portae Lucis*, 1516. Each Attribute is under the care of an Angel.

The Kabbalist

Imagine an icon as it might have existed in the mind of a Kabbalist scholar of fifteenth-century Toledo. A beam of light streams from the window onto his lectern and he looks up in reverie from his books to picture to himself the great Tree of the Angelic World.

First he recreates the bare abstract scheme of the ten Sefiroth, the ten Divine Attributes which govern and shape the universe both seen and unseen. They arrange themselves in a shape like a rose-bush on which ten measureless blossoms of light appear.

Now each of the roses of light will unfold its petals and reveal a winged figure. At the crown of the Tree appears the great Metatron, he who is closest to the Divine

Throne. This Angel was once the prophet Enoch 'who was not, for God had taken him up'. God set His own coronet on Enoch's head and gave him seventy-two wings and innumerable eyes. His flesh was transformed into flame, his sinews into fire, his bones into embers, and he is surrounded by storm, whirlwind, thunder and lightning.

The highest of all Angels, Metatron is a prophet, ancient, bearded, inspired; yet at the same time an eternal and celestial adolescent, radiantly beautiful. Isaiah saw him 'sitting upon a throne, high and lifted up, and his train filled the temple. Above him stood the Seraphim: each one had six wings; with twain he covered his face, and with twain he covered his feet, and with twain he did fly.' (Isaiah 5, 1–2)

Around Metatron stand the Kerubim:

> ... every one had four wings. And their feet were straight feet; and the sole of their feet was like the sole of a calf's foot; and they sparkled like the colour of burnished brass. And they had the hands of a man under their wings on their four sides ... Their wings were joined one to another ... As for the likeness of their faces, they four had the face of a man, and the face of a lion, on the right side; and they four had the face of an ox on the left side; they four also had the face of an eagle. (Ezekiel I, 4–10)

From these creatures pour streams of fiery sweat like rivers of lightning, and from the drops of this are produced multitudes of Angels (Daniel 7, 10).

The Three Angels on the left of the Tree are Zaphkiel, Angel of Contemplation; Samael, Angel of Evil, and Raphael, Angel of Healing. Samael is also called Satan, Lucifer, the Morning Star. If surprised to see him here, our Kabbalist recalls that Angels may possess many forms simultaneously. If Satan – in one decayed, gargantuan manifestation – occupies the frozen pit of Dante's lowest hell, he may also appear as the strangely elegant and sardonic adversary in the *Book of Job* who strolls about Heaven to play a game of chance with the Lord. On the Tree the Kabbalist envisions him in his original glory, blazing with jewels.

As for Raphael, he is the Divine Physician and also the patron of travellers: he wears a pilgrim's hat, carries a staff and water-gourd, or perhaps a vial of healing ointment.

The trunk of the Tree, beneath Metatron, displays three more figures of our Kabbalist's icon: Michael, Gabriel and Sandalphon. No words can do justice to the glory of Michael, who is patron of Israel, chief of the heavenly hosts, and, like his counterpart the Persian god Mithra, the sun in splendour. He may be pictured as a radiant winged warrior dressed in shining armour, piercing with his spear the writhing form of a serpent or dragon beneath his feet.

Gabriel, who commands Spiritual Wisdom, takes the form of a beautiful youth dressed in green embroidered silk, holding to his lips a gold horn.

Lastly, Sandalphon (whose name suggests the sound of approaching footsteps) is the Guardian Spirit, at once the chief and prototype of all guardian Angels. He stands at the foot of the Tree, upon the created world, but his height extends upwards throughout all the universe, and he is taller than any other 'by a journey of five hundred years'.

Left: a six-winged Seraph standing on one of the 'Wheels' (Ophanim), which are also Angels; from *Christian Iconography* by Adolphe Napoléon Didron, 1886.

Above: less anthropomorphic and therefore more conventionally visionary, this Seraph is attended by two fiery Ophanim. Sixth-century bronze mirror, found in Aleppo.

Right: Seraph with a message-scroll from an Anglo-Saxon manuscript now in the Bodleian Library, Oxford.

Angels of Grace

In most religions and mythologies, Angels are reassuring presences, bringing comfort and the promise of eternal life. As intermediaries between earthly and heavenly worlds, they are represented in human form but with supernatural attributes, at the same time recognizable and strange, familiar and transfigured.

In polytheistic religions like those of ancient Egypt or Greece, the line between gods and angels is a thin one. Christianity and Islam make a firmer distinction. Angels are manifestations of a God who does not show himself directly. The different aspects of God are associated with different Angels. Gabriel has a similar character in both Christianity and Islam. It is he who announces to Mary that she will bear the Christ Child, and who conducts Mohammed on his ascent to heaven.

At the end of all things, according to the Book of Revelation, a seven-headed serpent will swallow the waters of earth, sucking all time and all matter into the maw of chaos. But above everything will fly the Angel, promise of salvation beyond time itself. From a German medieval manuscript.

To the Greeks, Sleep and Death were angelic figures. On a 5th-century BC red-figured vase they carry a dead warrior from the battlefield of Troy to their palaces beneath the earth.

Christian imagery descends directly from classical. Here, on an 11th-century capital of the Romanesque church of Ste Hilaire at Poitiers, France, it is the soul of the dead man in bodily form which is raised by angelic hands and taken up to heaven.

10

Isis, the Protectress, Virgin and Mother, manifests herself as an Angel, her wings spread to enfold her worshipper in the sleep of unity. So powerful was this image that it long outlasted ancient Egypt. In a visionary 12th-century German manuscript (right), Hildegarde of Bingen and her nuns are cradled in the arms of an Angel as tall as a mountain, whose crown brushes heaven and whose wings beat like the vast slow movement of clouds.

Angelic protectors in Islam and in Christianity. A Turkish miniature shows an Angel carrying off a prince, a 'soul at peace' like a child in its mother's arms. William Blake's watercolour of 1808, inspired by Milton's *Paradise Lost*, takes us to the Garden of Eden before the Fall of Man, when two Angels watched over the sleep of the still innocent Adam and Eve.

The philosopher

Plato in the Phaedrus implies that both the gods and the souls of men are winged. But the being who above all others must be winged is the one who is neither god nor man, but an intermediary between the two, a messenger – in Hebrew, *malakh*, in Greek, *angelos*. According to Socrates, Eros is not, as others would have it, the beautiful beloved; rather he is the Spirit who inspires the lover, who gives the lover his divine madness. Eros is neither mortal nor immortal. He is a spirit who interprets and conveys messages back and forth between men and gods. 'God does not deal directly with man; it is by means of spirits that all the intercourse and communication of gods with men, both in waking life and in sleep, is carried on.'

Socrates relates the priestess Diotima's account of Love's origins. On Aphrodite's birthday, Contrivance, the son of Invention, grew drunk on nectar, and Poverty took advantage of this to seduce him and bear his child, who was Eros.

> He is always poor, and, far from being sensitive and beautiful, as most people imagine, he is hard and weather-beaten, shoeless and homeless, always sleeping out for want of a bed, on the ground, on doorsteps, and in the street . . . But, being also his father's son, he schemes to get for himself whatever is beautiful and good; he is bold and forward and strenuous, always devising tricks like a cunning huntsman; he yearns after knowledge and is full of resource and is a lover of wisdom all his life, a skilful magician, an alchemist.

Like the Angels of the Kabbala, Eros is a messenger, a spirit; he is winged; he is both Ancient of Days and a graceful boy. In other contexts, we shall see that Eros also acts as guide of the soul, the guardian or spiritual double of man, and that he represents both the spiritual master and the beloved, and that this synthesis gives him a claim to be regarded as a manifestation of the highest of all Angels.

But he also plays tricks and is something of a magician. Nothing in our angelic icon prepared us for this. Can an Angel be a trickster? In order to answer, we must extend our view beyond the Holy Land and Greece, where the word 'Angel' is known, and discovered whether Plato's archetype of the winged man or spirit can be found elsewhere; and if so, under what disguises.

Eros as described by Agathon in Plato's *Symposium*: a beautiful boy with rose and lyre, the image of the beloved. Back of an incised mirror, Etruscan, early 5th century BC; British Museum, London.

Opposite:
Ultimately, all religious ceremony is attributed to Angels, for the purpose of ritual is to transform the individual self into a 'court of Angels' in which every limb and faculty possesses its celestial guardian. Mohammed learned the Islamic prayers by imitating the inhabitants of paradise. This page is a 16th-century Turkish miniature.

Far left: 'Love's Luck' – 'shoeless and weatherbeaten', Eros makes his own fortune in the world – and thereby moves the world itself. From Peter Vischer the Younger, *Fortuna Amoris*; Erlangen, Graphische Sammlung der Universität.

Left: The power of Venus is love – thus her 'son' Cupid hovers over her head like a nimbus or aura or 'Glory'. Hellenistic terracotta statuette; Taranto, Museo Nazionale.

Below: Greek figure of Eros, from the Mahdra wreck. Appropriately enough, this apotheosis of young male beauty was dredged up from the bottom of the sea as the image is dredged up from the unconscious.

The shaman

The Campu shaman of eastern Peru sings with an eerie, distant voice which causes even his clothing to vibrate. The good spirits appear to him alone; they take human forms and dance. The hawk Koakiti appears as a winged man:

> *Tobacco, tobacco, pure tobacco*
> *It comes from the Riber's Beginning.*
> *Koakiti the hawk brings it to you.*
> *Its flowers are flying, tobacco.*
> *It comes to your aid ...*
> *Koakiti the hawk is its owner.*

Tobacco smoke is the magic bridge by which the soul of the shaman can ascend into the spirit-world; hence its value. The hummingbird spirits also appear as Angels:

> *Hummingbirds, hummingbirds, they come running*
> *Hummingbirds, hummingbirds, dark appearance*

A man's face in the belly of an eagle, symbolizing the ascendant and victorious mode of consciousness. Kwakiutl, Vancouver Island, Canada.

Hummingbirds, hummingbirds, all our brothers
Hummingbirds, hummingbirds, they all hover
Hummingbirds, hummingbirds, group without blemish.

Lame Deer, a contemporary Sioux medicine man, gives in his autobiography this description of the Four Thunderbirds, who are also winged men:

> . . . There are four large, old thunderbirds. The great *wakinyan* of the west is the first and foremost among them. He is clothed in clouds. His body has no form, but he has huge, four-jointed wings. He has no feet, but he has claws, enormous claws. He has no head, but he has a huge beak with rows of sharp teeth. His colour is black. The second thunderbird is red. He has wings with eight joints. The third thunderbird is yellow. The fourth thunderbird is blue. This one has neither eyes nor ears.

Thus, then, are the 'Kerubim', the 'four living creatures' of the Sioux.

He who has a vision of these beings must become a clown, a contrary-man or *heyoka*. He does everything backwards, to the amusement and often the horror of the tribe; like a medieval jester he has licence to turn the world topsy-turvy, to be a perpetual Lord of Misrule. The *heyoka* is also a prophet, a holy man: a sacred fool.

Raven (Qaq), the demiurge or agent of Chaos and Creation of the Tlingit of northwestern America, is another winged creature, a black, foul-mouthed, greedy, lecherous trickster who also brings light into the world by stealing the moon.

He knows who owns the moon: an old fisherman, sculling across the seas of utter darkness of 'olden times', keeps the source of light hidden inside ten boxes, like a Chinese puzzle, high on a shelf in his cabin.

Raven changes himself into a pine-needle and floats on the surface of a spring. The fisherman's daughter drinks the water, conceives and gives birth to a child. The fisherman dotes on his new grandchild and spoils him. The baby cries; the man offers him toy after toy, but only the moon-box pleases him. He opens all the boxes and plays with the bright ball. The fisherman suspects nothing and leaves the cabin.

At once Raven resumes his bird-form, utters the raven cry – 'Gaa!' – and flies up out of the smoke-hole, the moon in his beak. He breaks off bits of it and creates the sun and stars.

Another 'angelic' god, Hermes the messenger, becomes the Mercurius of the alchemists. He presides over the 'war' of duality and the 'marriage' of perfect union. From *Musaeum Hermeticum Reformatum et Amplificatum* . . . Frankfurt 1678.

Raven is Logos (born of a virgin); he is Lucifer and Prometheus, Light-bearers; Maya, the Hindu goddess of nature and illusion; and Proteus, the Greek god who assumes many shapes, the very soul of matter. He manifests as a bird, a beautiful boy, a terrifying old man with a beard of moss, an old woman with a beak-shaped nose. He is the first and greatest shaman, the man who penetrates the secrets, becomes a spirit-bird and flies up the tree after the light, cawing with wild laughter. He carves the first totem-pole, symbol of the World-Tree or Angelic Ladder, the hierarchy of the cosmos, record of his journey and heraldic emblem of his people. He is Metatron, the prophet who becomes an Angel, and Hermes the trickster with angelic features, messenger of the gods who steals the cattle of the sun and invents the lyre; also Mercurius of the alchemists, the winged and naked youth.

Fate is a messenger of the gods and hence winged. *Opposite:* Roman copy after a Greek original; Turin, Museo Lapidario.

Nike, or Victory (*left*), served as a model for Christian Angels; only he who meditates on truth is truly victorious. Antique stucco found in the Farnesina gardens; Rome, Museo Nazionale.

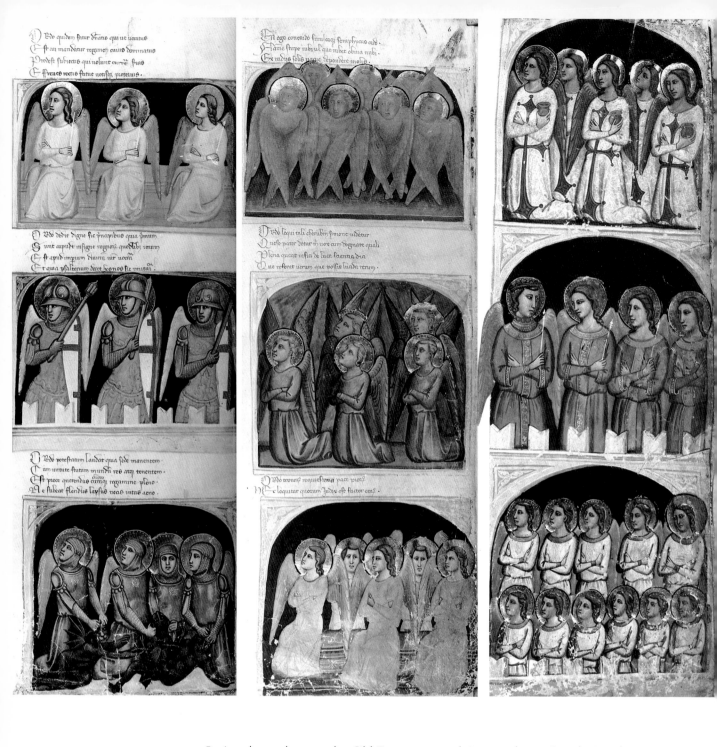

The nine Orders or Hierarchies of Angels, as described by Dionysius the Areopagite: Searaphim, Kerubim and Ophanim; Dominions, Virtues and Powers; Principalities, Archangels and Angels. From a 14th–century Italian address in Latin verse to Robert of Anjou, now in the British Library, London.

Basing themselves on the Old Testament and Apocrypha, artists depicted certain Angels in the form of Wheels, which Ezekiel first described: '. . . and their appearance and their work was as it were a wheel in the middle of a wheel.' (I, 16) They move through a firmament which is the colour of a 'terrible crystal', and around a throne like sapphire, on which sits Metatron, suffused in the radiance of the rainbow. The Wheels are often called 'Thrones', but are sometimes seen simply as the 'mounts' of the Kerubim or Seraphim.

Some of this imagery, to be seen in the sculpture of Chartres Cathedral, is drawn from the *Hierarchies* of Dionysius, which gives us descriptions of the nine Orders of the Angels. The biblical accounts of the first three, Seraphim, Kerubim and Wheels or

26

Thrones, have already been mentioned. The next three Orders, Dominions, Virtues and Powers, are described by Dionysius as wearing long albs, golden girdles and green stoles. They carry golden staves in their right hands and the seal of God in their left. The lowest Orders, Principalities, Archangels and Angels, dress in soldier's garb with golden belts and carry lance-headed javelins and hatchets. At Mount Athos, in the frescoes and inscriptions of the convent of Iviron, we discover more detail:

The *Seraphim* inflame mortals towards Divine love. They are red, and their three pairs of wings are red; their swords are red as flame. The *Kerubim*, possessors of wisdom, pour it forth in floods. They have a single pair of blue wings, and are richly garbed as Orthodox bishops.

Above all limit are set the high *Thrones* around the Most High. They are fiery Wheels with eyes and a haloed Angle's head. The Virgin is linked to this order: 'True Throne of God she exalts the Thrones of God'.

The *Dominions* direct their will in accordance with the truly supreme power of the absolute Master. They have two wings, robe, mantle, shoes. In the right hand they hold a seal with a monogram of Jesus, in the left a staff surmounted by a cross. St John the Baptist is depicted as one of this Order, but barefoot and clad in skins; for he was the messenger and Angel of Jesus.

Contrary to popular opinion, Islam does not prohibit images. Theologians may frown, but Moslem artists, like Sufi mystics, have imbibed a rich iconography of Angels from all the streams and sources which nourish the Islamic 'mythos': Jewish, Christian, Zoroastrian and Mesopotamian, Hermetic, Classical, pagan, Gnostic and Manichaean, Buddhist and shamanist. The following is an 'angelography', culled from various Islamic sources:

From the soles of his feet to his head, Israfil, the Angel of the Day of Judgment, has hairs and tongues over which are stretched veils. He glorifies Allah with each tongue in a thousand languages, and Allah creates from his breath a million Angels who glorify Him. Israfil looks each day and each night towards Hell, approaches without being seen and weeps; he grows thin as a bowstring and weeps bitter tears. His trumpet or horn has the form of a beast's horn and contains dwellings like the cells of a bee's honeycomb; in these the souls of the dead repose.

Mika'il (Michael) was created by Allah 5,000 years after Israfil. He has hairs of saffron from his head to his feet, and his wings are of green topaz. On each hair he has a million faces and in each face a million eyes and a million tongues. Each tongue speaks a million languages and from each eye fall 70,000 tears. These become the Kerubim who lean down over the rain and the flowers and the trees and the fruit.

Jibra'il (Gabriel) was created five hundred years after Mika'il. He has 1600 wings and hair of saffron. The sun is between his eyes and each hair has the brightness of the moon and stars. Each day he enters the Ocean of Light 360 times. When he comes forth, a million drops fall from each wing to become Angels who glorify Allah. When he appeared to the Prophet to reveal the Koran, his wings stretched from the East to the West. His feet were yellow, his wings green, and he wore a necklace of rubies or coral. His brow was light, his face luminous; his teeth were of a radiant brightness. Between his two eyes were written the words: There is no god but God, and Mohammed is the Prophet of God.

This 'Islamic' Angel displays Buddhist, Manichaean, Christian and Hellenistic influences. One of a pair of winged figures originally above the main entrance to the Citadel in Konya, 1220; Konya, Ince Minaret Museum.

The Angel as messenger in three traditions: Hellenistic, Christian and Islamic. Detail of Hebe from an antique vase painting; detail from *The Annunciation* by Melozzo da Forli; Moghul miniature showing an Angel appearing to an Indian ruler.

The Angel of Death, Azrael, is veiled before the creatures of God with a million veils. His immensity is vaster than the Heavens, and the East and West are between his hands like a dish on which all things have been set, or like a man who has been put between his hands that he might eat him, and he eats of him what he wishes; and thus the Angel of Death turns the world this way and that, just as men turn their money in their hands. He sits on a throne in the sixth Heaven. He has four faces, one before him, one on his head, one behind him and one beneath his feet. He has four wings, and his body is covered with innumerable eyes. When one of these eyes closes, a creature dies.

What do these and all Angels have in common? In both monotheistic and polytheistic traditions, Angels serve as messengers of God (or of the gods). We are

dealing with the inhabitants of an intermediate world, and the function of messenger is *par excellence* that of intermediary. According to the Prophet Mohammed, Angels are sent by God to earth to search out those places where individuals or groups are engaged in remembering or invoking the Deity. They listen with joy, hovering over the roofs of these humans who are fulfilling the task for which they were created: to know God, Who loves to be known. Then they fly back to the Divine Throne and repeat what they have heard (though God already knows it better than they) and are entrusted with blessings to bestow on earth.

This is what characterizes Angels in all traditions: they move between earth and heaven, like the figures seen in Jacob's vision of the ladder.

The Angel of the Lord

In the Bible, the Angel of the Lord obviously possesses a spiritual nature, but it also assumes physical characteristics as a voice or a vision. To the reader of myth, to the poet, this apparent contradiction presents no problem. But over the centuries certain theologians have furiously debated the question of how something lacking a material nature can take on a shape. The medieval Jewish philosopher Maimonides reduced all apparitions recorded in Scripture to mere 'figurative expressions', or allegories. Other theologians insisted that the 'incorporeality' of Angels did not rule out their being created of some kind of subtle or ideal matter, so that they are bodiless but numerical. Aquinas called them 'powers' and 'immaterial spirits'. If Scripture refers to their manifestation, he maintained, we must think of it as 'a succession of contacts of power at diverse places' in time but not in location.

Theologians, philosphers and mystics all have the right to define the Angel however they choose, and all such insights can be valuable. But precisely because there are so many different definitions, it will be simpler and more profitable to begin by asking not 'What is an Angel?' but 'What does an Angel do?' Myth and Scripture more often yield stories than definitions, more concerned with function than philosophy.

Certain Angels remain forever immersed in the contemplation of divine beauty, unaware even that God created Adam. Although these are the highest Angels, they remain outside the hierarchy. The highest Angel actually belonging to the hierarchy is called the Angel of the Lord – or sometimes simply 'the Lord'.

In the Old Testament he is mentioned many times. It is he who speaks from the burning bush, saves Shadrach, Meshach and Abednego from the fiery furnace, appears as the god of Beth-el in Jacob's dream and stands in the way of Balaam's ass. The three Angels entertained by Abraham at Mamre appear as a triple manifestation of this 'Lord' and are thus identified by Christians as 'the Old Testament trinity', a prefiguration of Father, Son and Holy Ghost.

We have already met this Angel under his Kabbalistic description and name: Metatron, 'Closest to the Throne'. Another Kabbalistic name is Phanuel, 'Divine Face'. 'My face shall go before thee', as God promises Moses in *Exodus*.

As St Augustine puts it, the Lord (as God) is 'in' the Angel, who is therefore rightly called 'Lord'. 'It is the name of the indweller, not the temple.' But in truth, as Gabriel told Mohammed, God is veiled by 70,000 veils of light and darkness, and if these were suddenly swept aside, 'even I would be utterly consumed.' The absolute in its absoluteness cannot be contemplated. Therefore every manifestation of God, every epiphany, must take the form suited to the heart which beholds it.

In the Sufi system of Abdul Karim Jili, the highest Angel is identified with 'The Spirit' mentioned in the Koran. He is made from God's light, and 'from him God created the world and made him His organ of vision of the world.' He is the Divine Command, chief of the Kerubim, axis of creation. He has eight major forms, great Angels who bear the Throne, and all other Angels are created from him 'like drops from the ocean'. He is also the eternal 'prophetic light' from which all prophets derive their inner being; the breath or spirit sent to Mary to conceive Jesus; and Mohammed in his perfect manifestation.

Abraham plays host to three Angels at Mamre. They are portrayed here in a 13th-century Bible in St John's College, Cambridge, as a three-headed figure presaging the Christian Trinity.

Angelic Choirs

According to medieval theologians, reflected in sources as far apart as Dante's *Divine Comedy* and the *Koran*, God created the Universe and everything in it, not in order to increase his power and goodness, which are by definition infinite, but in order that other beings should share in his love.

This is the meaning of the angelic choirs who are represented hymning the glory of God. Music-making is particularly appropriate to Angels, whose dance can become a mandala of paradise. But music by itself lacks one particularly angelic function: the word, or Logos. Thus it is in poetry, defined as rhythmic speech accompanied by music, that man reaches the language of the Angels, or as the sufis call it, the language of the birds, revealed by the djinn to Solomon. Rhythm lifts time out of the realm of the profane and transmutes it into the *Aevum*, the 'created eternity' of the Angels.

As the Christian image of Angels evolved from the classical they became more ethereal and beautiful. The Virgin Mary was often shown sitting in a garden (the 'hortus conclusus' of the Song of Songs) which is itself a sort of paradise populated by rejoicing Angels. She is the Queen of Angels, the most perfect of the intermediaries between heaven and earth. This is a detail from a 15th-century painting by Stefano da Zevio at Verona.

The Orders of Angels are also
Choirs, for they preside over all
the arts and especially over
music, the most disembodied
and hence spiritual of all creative
modes. Simon Marmion (right)
and Sandro Botticelli (far right)
were among the Renaissance
artists who fixed music-making
Angels in the popular
imagination. Botticelli's Angels
are supernatural beings hymning
the Mystic Nativity.

34

Apsaras in Hindu mythology form an angelic mandala on the ceiling of an Indian palace (above). It is a round dance, a circle of paradise, an evocation of spring, a diagram of ecstasy to gaze up at, intoxicating the spectator by the sky-whirling choreography. In the same position, on a vault of the cathedral of Cefalù, Sicily, kerubim and seraphim divide all space between them in the universal four-sided formula of the mandala — an artistic device to trigger realization in the contemplative soul.

In a 15th-century Islamic miniature by
Mi'raj-nameh (below), Mohammed,
visiting heaven, is awestruck by the
cosmic form of the Archangel Gabriel,
who had previously appeared to him
only as a disembodied voice or as a
human youth. Right: an early medieval
miniature illustrating the Apocalypse.
The Angel with the millstone reduces
every grain of separative existence to
the dust of divine union – the end of
time.

The Logos

The Eastern Church Fathers solve the problem of the Lord/Angel of the Lord in a different way. God is three Persons, and the Person or aspect of God which manifests itself, which appears on the level of creation, is neither the Father nor the Holy Spirit, but the Son. 'In the beginning was the Word,' the Logos, the Christic Principle. All Old Testament appearances of the Lord/Angel of the Lord are considered by the Eastern theologians to have been partial manifestations, limited theophanies of the Logos. Jesus is the final and perfect incarnation of the Logos; He is the Living Word, the Word made flesh.

If the Logos has a special Angel, however, it must surely be Gabriel. It is he who announces to Mary the descent of the spirit; it is he who brings to Mohammed the words of the Koran. He has several forms: in his 'cosmic' manifestations to Mohammed he is awe-inspiring, his body blots out half the sky, which resounds with the rushing of his wings. In icons and late medieval paintings, however, he takes his more usual shape, that of a delicate and uncannily beautiful youth, in which he often appeared to Mohammed. The Sufi Ruzbehan Baqli describes him: 'In the first rank I saw Gabriel, like a maiden, or like the moon amongst the stars. His hair was like a woman's, falling in long tresses. He wore a red robe embroidered in green ... He is the most beautiful of Angels ... His face is like a red rose.'

In every tradition Gabriel possesses a feminine beauty, symbolic of the perfection and bliss which are the very essence of his 'message'. Detail of the Ghent altarpiece by Jan and Hubert van Eyck.

Opposite:
The empyrean of Apocalypse echoes with music; a peacock-angel opens a mandorla in the sky, in which Christ and the symbols of the four Evangelists are displayed. On this night of nights, the one who wakes might easily out-do Jacob and climb to heaven on a ladder of light. From the Bamberg *Apocalypse*, 15th century.

The Annunciation to Mary. In the shade of Jesse's Tree, where David plays his harp, the dove seems almost conjured out of Heaven, as if Gabriel were a benign sorcerer. Detail from the Westphalia Passion Altar, c.1400.

The Islamic version of the Annunciation differs from the Christian one only in dress; the Koran is quite specific on the subject of the Virgin Birth and Mary's preeminence. Illumination from an Islamic treatise on different systems of chronology, 1307.

According to many Islamic thinkers, Gabriel is the tenth and last of the great chain of Archangel intellects which emanate from God. He rules the sphere of the moon and all that lies below it; hence he is the Angel of Humanity. All 'terrestrial Angels' – human souls – derive from him. In a sense he is father, in another sense beloved. Gabriel is the archon of all Guardian Angels. When an Angel appears to man, he is Gabriel, or is sent by Gabriel.

If the Angel is a 'messenger', moving between heaven and earth 'with a lightly rushing motion' (as Plato says), he is not merely a *nuncio*, a character out of the prologue of a Greek play. He *is* the Message, as the Message manifests itself to man.

Thus the philosopher Philo Judeaus calls all Angels *logoi*. In interpreting the story of Balaam's ass, he names the Angel '*Conviction*, the divine logos, the Angel who guides our feet and removes the obstacles before them, that we may walk without stumbling along the high road.'

So the logos-Angel appears often bearing a book, or somehow he *is* a book or a letter. The Gnostics named him 'the Call', the summons from beyond the spheres which awakens the soul from her profitless slumber, her demonic dream, and beckons her upwards to her true home. According to the Hebrew *Testament of Naphtali*, the Angels taught the nations of man their various languages; and for the Sufi each of the twenty-eight letters of the Arabic alphabet is ruled by an Angel (and is related to a phase of the moon, Gabriel's sphere).

Sophia

For the most part, Angels are either male – since they represent the Active Intellect in relation to the human soul seen as passive and feminine – or androgynous, since they represent perfection, completion, *coincidentia oppositorum*. But the feminine cannot be excluded from the realm of the 'Most High'. In the Kabbala, the second of the Sefiroth (or 'universal Divine principles'), *Binah* or Wisdom, is feminine. If Western monotheism has a 'goddess', then this is she.

She is often called by her Greek name, Sophia, Wisdom – that which the philosophers love. In Orthodox Christianity she occupies an exalted position, related but not equivalent to that of the Virgin. The iconographers paint her as a winged Angel seated upon a throne. She is crimson, the colour of alchemical stone, or of twilight, the time which opens a crack in time, a gateway between worlds.

In the grandiose cosmic speculations of early Christian gnosis, the theme of Sophia is amplified and distorted in strange and revealing ways. True dualistic gnosis, like that of the second-century philosopher Valentinus, is based on the idea of a complete separation of Good and Evil. Good lies entirely *outside* the cosmos; creation is totally evil, ruled by diabolical powers. The God of religion is often depicted as one of these demons; the gnostics particularly detested the Jehovah of the Old Testament, and taught that Christ came to release man from bondage imposed by this false god of the Jews.

Thus the values of the Old Testament are reversed as in a carnival mirror, and Sophia is revealed as the spirit responsible, through her *folly*, for the creation of the world, an error of cataclysmic proportions.

The Archangels and Satan

The gnostic 'shadows' of the Archangels are seven planetary demons. This numeration occurs for perhaps the first time in the ancient religion of Babylonia where the winged bull-man carved over and over again in monolithic grandeur by Mesopotamian and Persian artists exhibits the archaic and totemic countenance of the Angel.

Nebo, the Minister of Merodach, is the Angel of the Lord. The moon-god Athar stands at the head of a heavenly host, the Igigi, whose champion in Ninip. The Angel-messengers are called Sukalli, sons of the deity whose vicegerents they are. These and other names written on clay tablets long buried in dust, and crumbling slowly back into the element from which they were moulded, call up for us the magic

Ahura Mazda, chief of the Assyrian pantheon, is portrayed in angelic form in this relief from Khorsabad, now in the Louvre, and on one of the palace gateways of Persepolis (*far right*).

'sidereal piety' of the Chaldeans, the Harranians, the Sabeans, the star worshippers, our own past selves. Only one tiny Gnostic sect still survives today, the Mandaeans of the Mesopotamian marshes, followers of an unrecognizable John the Baptist who was betrayed by Jesus. Their books are incised on metal. Everything else, all starry wisdom and occult Angelic names, is vanished.

Zoroaster transformed these ancient gods into Archangels. By the time the Jews came in their exile to the East, his religion held sway, and much of the Jewish and Christian lore of Angels dates from Israel's contact with 'Babylonian' wisdom.

The seven Zoroastrian Amesh-spentas include God the Most High seen as a winged sun-disc, a supreme Angel of Pure Light: Ahura-Mazda. Beneath him are six Archangels.

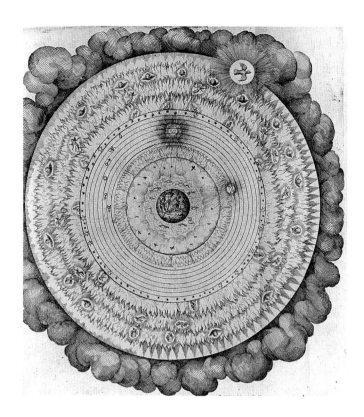

The nature of Heaven

In the Western tradition, Heaven usually consists of seven spheres to correspond with the seven planets. Under the influence of Gnosticism (which sometimes spoke of 360 heavens, all evil), some cosmographers removed the spiritual world outside the 'heavenly' spheres. Planetary symbolism was used with power and precision as late as Dante.

The lowest Jewish heaven contains clouds, winds, the 'Upper Waters' (symbolic of the gateway to the Imaginal World), two hundred Angels of the stars, storehouses of snow, ice and dew with their guardian Angels. The second is dark and full of sinners awaiting Judgment. The third contains Eden, with three hundred Angels of Light, and Gehenna or Hell (which is depicted as subterranean usually only when the earth is thought of as flat, although Dante combined the two symbolic systems in a brilliant tour de force of cosmography). In the fourth heaven are the chariots of Sun, Moon and Stars, and great Winds in the shapes of a phoenix and brazen serpent with lions' heads (reminiscent of the Mithraic Aeons). In the fifth the fallen Angels languish in silence and despair. In the sixth reside seven Kerubim with hosts of radiant Angels who control the influences of the stars, along with the Angels of Time, the seas, rivers, crops and the souls of mankind. The seventh contains ineffable Light, Archangels, Kerubim, Seraphim and Ophanim (Thrones or Wheels).

Corresponding to the seven heavens are seven earths, the highest of which is our own world; and each of these fourteen levels is hooked like a chain-link to the ones above and below it. God presides over all; every day He mounts a Kerub and visits

The structure of the Macrocosm: creation is ordered, both in and beyond time and space, into ontological levels or layers of reality. The Ptolemaic universe from Robert Fludd, *History of the Macrocosm*, 1617.

48

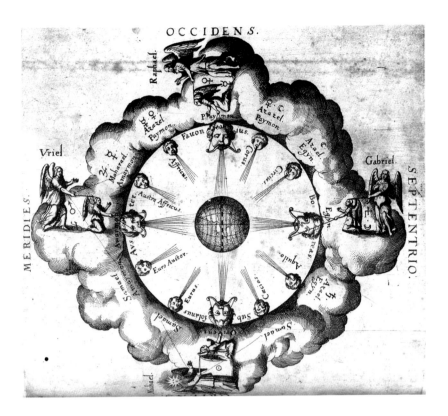

each of the planes, receiving homage; at dusk He returns on high on the wings of the wind.

The elements of this myth receive further implification from Moslem visionaries such as Jili. His first heaven is that of the Moon. The Holy Spirit is here, 'so that this heaven might have the same relation to earth as Spirit to body.' Adam dwells here in silvery-white light. The second heaven is that of Mercury (identified by the sufis with the Egyptian Hermes, the prophets Idris and Enoch). Here the Angels of the arts and crafts reside bathed in grey luminousness. The third heaven, that of Venus, is created from the Imagination and is the locale of the World of Similitudes, the subtle forms of all earthly things, the source of dreams and visions. The prophet Joseph lives here in yellow light. The heaven of the Sun is created from the Light of the Heart; Israfil presides over the host of prophets in a golden glow. The heaven of Mars, of the death-Angel Azrael, is blood-red with the Light of Judgment. That of Jupiter is blue with the Light of Spiritual Power (*himma*) and is lorded over by Michael. Here reside the Angels of mercy and blessing, shaped as animals, birds and men; others appear, in Jili's words, 'as substances and accidents which bring health to the sick, or as solids and liquids which supply created things with food and drink. Some are made half of fire and half of ice. Here resides Moses, drunk on the wine of the revelation of Lordship.' The seventh heaven is that of Saturn, the first to be created – from the substance of the First Intelligence – and it consists of Black Light (symbolic of *fana'*, Annihilation in the Divine Oneness).

Jili also speaks of seven earths or 'climes' inhabited by men, djinn and devils. The seventh is a Hyperborean paradise beyond Mount Qaf (the *axis mundi*) untouched by the Fall and ruled by Khezr, the Green Man or Hidden Prophet.

Space itself is both material and spiritual; the Archangels who preside over the directions also rule the 'winds', the breath of the Spirit. The Four Archangels and the Twelve Winds from Robert Fludd, *Medicina Catholica*, 1629.

The Cosmos is a mirror in which each facet reflects the face of Divine reality; each of the planets, zodiacal houses and spatial directions is thus presided over or identical with an angel which represents some aspect of God's plenitude of being. Mirror of Life; a Persian manuscript in the Topkapi Saray Museum, Istanbul.

Opposite: the Angel as Preserver, or Axis Mundi, Pole of the World; the very earth would not remain in place without the intervention of that cosmic force which is Love. A 9th-century mosaic in the vault of the Church of Santa Prassede, Rome.

Space and time

They, all together, singing in harmony and moving around the heaven in their measured dance, unite in one harmony whose cause is one and whose end is one: it is this harmony which entitles the All to be called 'order' and not disorder.

DE MUNDO, ANON., FIRST CENTURY

The Old Testament mentions Angels of Nations; some Biblical commentators say that there are seventy, others as many as the tribes or even the cities of men. 'When the Most High gave nations their homes and set the divisions of men, He fixed the borders of peoples according to the numbers of divine beings' (Qumran fragment). Like the tutelary deities of paganism, the *genii loci*, the river-gods, mountain sprites and wood-nymphs of Ovid's *Metamorphoses*, these Angels protect their places – but in a deeper sense they *are* these places. They are the inspiration, the aesthetic shock, sensed by visionary, poet, artist, hermit or traveller.

The Christian theologian Origen, writing in the third century, explains that the Angels of Nations are sometimes perceived as gods, and are responsible for the fact that each religion possesses Truth: 'The secret and occult philosphy of the Egyptians, the astrology of the Chaldeans, the Hindu claims pertaining to the science of the Most High God . . . Each of these princes has a separate science and a special doctrine to teach.' Other Christian theologians claim that the missions of these Angels have been superseded by that of Christ; but one might seize on Origen's ideas as a justification for a more universal approach to comparative religion.

Of all the higher Archangels, Michael seems to have most often 'condescended' to play the role of an Angel of place. Not only does he rule Heaven, he also protects Israel and battles against the Angels of Israel's enemies. In Egypt he is the patron of the Nile, and his feast is celebrated on the day the river rises. In Germany the newly-converted pagans recognized Michael as the god Woden, and transformed his mountain shrines into churches of the Archangel. He is the Patron of Brittany and Cornwall, where Mont-Saint-Michel and Michael's Mount bear witness to the Angel's taste for imposing scenery and exquisite architecture.

Since *The Book of Revelation* tells us that Michael battled with the dragon, he has been linked to many of the European, Celtic and Middle Eastern myths of mountains and dragons (unless the stories are told of his earthly 'avatar' St George). Just as in alchemy the volatile spirit of mercury must be 'milled' or fixed by the stable solar principle of sulphur, so the lithe and sinuous dragon, slippery as quicksilver, must be 'slain' by the Angel of the Sun, Michael. The symbolism is this: the vital spirit is by nature chaotic and chthonic, but the intellect cannot operate without its power. To 'kill' the dragon is not to eliminate it but to tame it, to leash it, to order it, to use its power towards spiritual ends.

The guardian Angel of Portugal also seems to have some connection with Michael. King Manoel I (1495–1521) petitioned the Pope to sanction the Feast of the Angel of Portugal on the third Sunday in July; no other country has such an observance. Alfonso Henriques founded a chivalric Order of the Wing in Honour of Michael (who is the Angel of chivalry) to commemorate his victory over the Saracens at Santarem,

when his flagging forces were revived by the apparition of a hand grasping a sword, and a wing, emerging from thin air before their ranks.

The Angel of Portugal appeared as recently as 1916 to the three children of Fatima to prepare them for the apparitions of Mary in 1917. He took the form of a young man brilliant as crystal when it is lit by the sun, holding a chalice and a host dripping blood.

If the Angels 'penetrate' the earth to such an extent that one can call the Earth itself an Angel, they themselves are not in space in the same sense as men. As Aquinas says, 'Each of the spiritual entities . . . is the whole of the sphere of its heaven, yet at the same time has a particular place, different from that of its companions . . . for they are not bodies, nor is the heaven in question a body.'

St Michael and his warrior Angels conquering Satan in the form of a dragon; a woodcut from Albrecht Dürer's *Apocalypse*, 1498.

Warrior Angels

The myth of Satan, the Fallen Angel, is the Christian and Islamic way of reconciling dualism with an omnipotent God. Satan, God's own creation, rebels against God, necessitating an order of warrior Angels led by Michael to defeat him. He then introduces sin into the world and becomes the minister of God's punishment, presiding over hell, the place of eternal torment. All this has to be seen as an allegory of separation from God, but in traditional Christian art the imagery assumes a graphically literal form.

In conjunction with the vision of the Apocalypse, this gave the angelic order a new role – that of defending God's throne and consigning the damned to hell. St Michael becomes a symbol of the eternal triumph of good over evil, with Satan as a dragon or mythical monster. The moment of death is particularly critical, the moment when good and bad Angels battle for the dying man's soul.

Angels have a traditional role in Christian mythology as executioners of God's judgment, raising the saved to heaven and thrusting the damned into hell. This detail is from a mosaic of the Last Judgment in Torcello Cathedral, Italy. Traditional religion stresses the image of the Last Judgment, sinners confirmed forever to the flames. But how can God, who is both One and Good, perpetuate a separateness and an evil? The answer is that the 'last judgment' takes place only on the level of the microcosm, the individual awareness. In the macrocosm, in God, all souls are 'saved'.

Traditionally, St Michael is the warrior Angel who overcomes Satan, often represented in the form of a dragon, as on the 12th-century tympanum of St Michel d'Etraignes, Angoulême, France. On another Romanesque tympanum, at Autun (right), an Angel weighing the soul of a dead man holds down the scales on the side of salvation, while a grimacing demon on the other side fails to tip the balance the other way.

Overleaf:
Two more images of St Michael defeating the Dragon, the pattern of the true knight of chivalry. One is from an 11th-century Gospel book, the other a Coptic icon. Solar, chivalrous, victorious day overcomes lunar, watery, reptilian night. The serpent is cast out of the garden not once but countless times. Whenever a soul triumphs over itself Michael is present.

'And the second Angel sounded, and as it were a great mountain burning with fire was cast into the sea, and the third part of the sea became blood': the Blowing of the Second Trumpet of Revelation, illustrated (far left) in an early 14th-century *Apocalypse*.

St Michael's role as angelic hero defeating Satan (shown left in a detail from a painting by Petrus Christus, 15th century) is described in the same book: 'And there was war in heaven; Michael and his Angels fought against the dragon; and the dragon fought, and his Angels, and prevailed not; neither was their place found any more in heaven. And the great dragon was cast out, called the Devil and Satan, which deceiveth the whole world; he was cast into the earth, and his Angels were cast out with him.'

Angelic eroticism

Contact with the Intermediate World sometimes involves a certain sexual ambiguity, an exalted erotic state often interpreted by monotheistic puritans as diabolic. Archaic societies tolerated a balancing measure of chaos: the Saturnalia. Along with the sacred clown, such societies also recognized and even enjoyed the psychic necessity for manifestations of non-ordinary sexuality. Temple prostitution is one example, shamanic homosexuality another. Both occur among the Dyak of Borneo, who say that since the earth is feminine and the sky masculine, the shamans who intermediate between the two should act out this cosmic ambiguity in sexual terms, the men as hermaphrodites, the women as prostitutes. Similar ideas are found in ancient Japanese and contemporary Sioux cultures, among others.

Actual contact with spirits is often sexual: the shaman 'marries' his guardian spirit and must cohabit with it despite its terrifying appearance. In the Hermetic tract, *Isis the Prophetess to her Son Horus*, the prophetess relates how an Angel dwelling above the firmament came down, made love to her, and revealed to her the hidden mysteries of the preparation of gold and silver.

The *Book of Numbers* briefly relates that in the days before Noah the 'sons of God' came down to earth to teach the secrets of the arts to mankind, and that they fell in love with and married the beautiful daughters of men. Apparently no condemnation is intended, since the offspring of these unions are called 'the heroes of days gone by, the famous men'. The shamanic origins of this tale are hinted at in the Midrashim (traditional commentaries on scripture), which relate that these Angels revealed the Hidden Name of God to a girl named Istehar, who was thus able to ascend to heaven.

The Book of Enoch, however, interprets the incident as the origin of evil. Two hundred sons of God, under the leadership of one called Semjaza, descended without Divine permission, 'defiled' human women and 'taught them charms and enchantments, and the cutting of roots ... and they became pregnant and bare great giants, whose height was three thousand ells [11,250 feet]!... The giants turned against men and devoured them.' Azazel taught men the arts of war and women the vanity of cosmetics. Fornication and lawlessness spread over the earth. Finally God ordered Michael to overcome these Angels, who are called 'Watchers', described by Enoch as 'stars whose privy members were like those of horses'. Enoch is rapt up in heaven to be told of God's displeasure, and of His intention to imprison the fallen Angels 'till the day of Judgment'.

At the centre of Angelic eroticism is the great Angel, Eros. In India he appears exactly as in Greece, a boy with bow and arrows (made of flowers and bees). According to the legend, Parvati, daughter of the god Himalaya, falls in love with Shiva. But the great god remains immersed in contemplation and refuses to notice her. Meanwhile the other gods interest themselves in Parvati's plight, because a terrible demon is ravaging the cosmos, and Brahma predicts that only a son of Shiva and Parvati can overcome this menace.

The hermaphrodite, symbol of the union of opposites; woodcut from *Rosarium Philisophorum*, printed as second part of *De Alchimia Opuscula*, 1550.

Opposite:
For Blake, Satan is only accidentally the cause of evil (since evil has no being in itself, but only as a deprivation of good). For the soul freed of illusion, the devil resumes his original Archangelic glory, his solar and energizing power.

Opposite: in Hindu Tantra, the feminine principle is sometimes seen as active, the masculine as passive; this enigmatic piece of Hellenistic carved marble may signify a similar doctrine in Greek paganism.

Left: the Greek Eros; a statuette from the 1st century BC.

Below: winged Eros; relief from a shrine of Eros and Aphrodite, Greek, end 2nd-century BC.

So Kama (Eros) is sent, with his wife Rati, to move Shiva's heart with desire for Parvati. But just as the boy is about to release his love-arrow, Shiva opens his third eye and with his terrible gaze burns Kama to ashes (hence his title, Ananga, the Bodiless). Rati (Passion) weeps, but hears a voice say, 'Thy lover is not lost forever; when Shiva weds Parvati he will restore Love's body to his soul.'

Finally Parvati wins Shiva's love by practising meditation and austerity. The wedding takes place, and all the prophecies are fulfilled.

The burning of Love's body signifies the predominance of contemplation over mere desire. But Parvati loves even when Love itself is destroyed, for she loves Wisdom. The restoration of Kama as a wedding gift from Shiva to his bride indicates that Love under the rule of Wisdom is true pleasure, ananda, Bliss. These motifs remind us of the great Western legend of Love, *Cupid and Psyche*, as told in the *Golden Ass* by the Neoplatonist and worshipper of Isis, Apuleius.

The story begins *before* the descent of the soul, Psyche, into the world. Beautiful and pure, she is potentially divine, 'a second Venus'. Aphrodite herself, however, portrayed in this tale as the illusory power of the world (Maya in Hinduism), cannot bear to think of a soul's remaining untouched by her wiles. She inspires an oracle to predict that Psyche will be married to a dreadful serpent, and then sends Cupid to make the girl fall in love with the ugliest creature he can find. All this symbolizes the 'fall' of the soul into the corrupt material world.

But Cupid himself falls in love with her, for Love without an object of love is incomplete, and the Soul is made for Love. Thus her marriage (i.e., birth) is not into a nightmare but into a dream of love. Psyche cannot see Cupid (he is 'bodiless') for she has not yet earned the right to true vision; nevertheless he visits her every night and her life is happy at first, as childhood is magically happy, because it is simple. Psyche's sisters (her bad inner faculties, her 'ego') are pictured as evil, but their action is not entirely so: they spur Psyche towards a new kind of maturity, a desire to know the object of her love. (As Mohammed said, 'He who knows himself, knows his Lord' — so he who knows his Lord, must know himself.)

Psyche tries to discover her lover's identity, an act of disobedience that results in her first true vision. Now she realizes how beautiful divinity really is, and also the extent of her own separation from it. She is now a seeker; she has entered on the spiritual path.

Interestingly, the only god who gives her good advice is Pan, spirit of wildness, who tells her not to weep or slay herself 'but rather adore and worship the great god Cupid and win him unto you, that is a delicate and wanton youth, by your gentle promise of service.'

Like a true aspirant, Psyche interprets this to mean 'worship *all* the gods'. Thus when Venus-as-Illusion sends her on her impossible tasks (all symbolizing the development of certain spiritual faculties), Psyche is aided by the gods themselves. Finally she descends into Hell ('Die before you die') — and the reward is a new vision of Cupid, who helps her to overcome her final test, and subdue her ego.

And Psyche gains immortality, is taken up to heaven like Elias and married to her love, who is Love himself, the beauty of the Divine And their child is the god Pleasure — *ananda* — Bliss.

The sexual bliss depicted in Tibetan art, as in this painting of a Mahasiddha, or Great Magus, with his dakini, symbolizes the perfection of spiritual union, the *coincidentia oppositorum*.

69

Angel Musicians; detail of panels
for an organ gallery by Hans
Memlinc (c.1430–1494); Musée
des Beaux-Arts, Antwerp.

A celestial attendant making
music. Indian carving, Victoria
and Albert Museum, London.

The Muse

The venerable Bede tells us that the poet Caedmon began his career unable to utter a word. When, in the evenings, the villagers would pass round the harp and sing, he would steal off to the hills in shame. One such night an Angel appeared to him and ordered him to sing; at once his lips were unlocked and he became a poet.

The function of the Muses for the poet Hesiod is that of the Angels for the Israelites: to reveal the cosmogony, the story of the origins of men and gods and the world. Indeed, Origen discourses on the tradition that Angels were involved in the very beginnings of language itself: not just Scripture, but all words are 'revealed'.

In primordial societies, shamans act as repositories of language, of rare, antique and special vocabularies often far more vast than those in ordinary usage. Their ecstasies are invariably preceded and accompanied by poetic recitals, and the epic and oral poetry of all peoples derive ultimately from the shaman's or hero's voyage to the Other World; or from possession, the descent of spirits into this world; or from the voices of the dead, the ancestors who have become spirits.

The Celts attained what might be called, in this respect, a high shamanic civilization. The functions of bard, seer and priest were related but highly specialized, and the techniques of ecstasy were attuned to the vast learning of bardic colleges in which the acquisition of a 'degree' could involve half a lifetime of study and preparation. The costume of the ancient Irish bard consisted largely of feathers: the poet as bird/man, the poet as Angel, or direct disciple of the Angel, Muse, White Goddess.

In Persia, lyric poetry revolves around the figure of the beloved. Poets like Rumi composed in a state of ecstasy (whirling round a pillar). Even today the Iranian musical modes correspond precisely to poetic metres, so that all traditional poetry can still be chanted. Some scholars believe in a connection between the twelve modes and the signs of the Zodiac and the twelve Angels of the months.

Some might call music the Angelic art; and in the sense that it approaches 'pure' spirit, this is true. Indeed, music in itself must also derive from the Other World, and provide a link between men and those choirs of beings who are depicted in Buddhist, Christian and Islamic art as singing and playing the lute or harp. All primordial musical instruments were revealed to men by spirits; the lyre was invented by Hermes, the messenger of gods. The drums of Siberian shamans are their divine horses, on which they ride the clouds; the drums of the Africans and Haitians are gods, carved out of pure spiritual substances mysteriously manifest in certain sacred trees. The *Ave Maria*, the words of Gabriel to Mary, are set in plainsong modes which seem sliced out of eternity; and St John Chrysostom tells us that the *Sanctus* is the chant of the Seraphim, 'reserved for the initiates, the baptized.'

Angel with lyre; fragment of Samian ware bowl-moulds, Arezzo Museum.

The Guardian Angel

For He hath given His Angels charge over thee, to keep thee in all thy ways.

PSALM 90

I go to meet my image and my image comes to meet me: it caresses and embraces me as if I were returning from captivity. MANDAEAN LITURGY OF THE DEAD

When man opens his heart, for even an instant, the figure he perceives (or the intuition he receives) is his Guardian Angel. When he hears the call to the spiritual life, when his psychic substance is protected from evil, when he meets certain mysterious figures in dreams, or even in waking day, who act out for him the drama of his own inner life – this is the Guardian Angel at work.

'It is a teaching of Moses that every believer has an Angel to guide him as a teacher and a shepherd' (St Basil); and Christ says of 'the little ones' that their 'Angels in heaven always behold the face of the Father.' In Zoroastrian belief, the soul after death meets a beautiful maiden who announces, 'I am none other than thine own personal conscience. Thou hast loved me in this form of sublimity, goodness and beauty in which I now appear unto thee.' At the time of his ordination a Taoist master is assigned a guardian spirit, called a *pen-ming*, which acts as a special liaison official to present the priest's documents and prayers to the lords of the cosmos. Some authors (including Philo) believe that each soul possesses a good and a bad Angel, who contend throughout life for its possession.

Joseph's Dream; from the Book of Pericopes of St Erentrud, Salzburg School, 1150–75.

Gnosticism provides a useful definition of the guardian: the Angel and the soul form a *syzygy* or 'pair'. The Angel is the soul's twin, its spiritual counterpart which 'sees the Father in heaven'. When St Anthony was starving alone in the desert he saw someone who looked exactly like him, fishing in a brackish pool; it was Anthony's guardian, showing him how to obtain food. Great prophets or saints may have great Archangels for their guardians, since their earthly missions involve the spiritual welfare of whole segments of mankind. 'The prophet hastens to accomplish the action which the Angels contemplate spiritually' (St Hilary). Thus Mohammed's guardian is Gabriel, and Arjuna's in a sense is Krishna, who chooses the great hero as a vehicle for the teachings enshrined in the *Bhagavad Gita*.

Great mystics are sometimes initiated by Angels rather than human masters. St Francis was protected by one of the Seraphim, who gave him the Stigmata. King Solomon and Padmasambhava (founder of Tibetan Buddhism) were both served by hordes of Angels, djinn, converted demons and fairies.

If – as St Thomas Aquinas claims – each Angel is a separate species, how can we mere individuals attain such a one-to-one relationship with an Angel? One possibility is that the guardians are in fact multiple manifestations of a single 'Angel of Humanity' (Sandalphon, or Gabriel).

The guardian is also in a sense the Beloved. The Persian philosopher Avicenna, speaking of the Angel, explains that 'the soul must grasp the beauty of the object that it loves; the image of that beauty increases the ardour of love; this ardour makes the soul look upward . . . Thus imagination of beauty causes ardor of love, love causes

St Francis is called 'seraphic'. In this miniature from a manuscript of the Golden Legend, compiled c.1300 by Jacobus de Voragine, he is seen receiving the stigmata from a Seraph.

74

lucuf leo num
ubi danuel miffuf fina œubbu
cuc poftaun fill
pfun diun

desire, and desire causes motion' on the level both of the spheres (which are drawn in love toward their Archangel-Intellects) and of human souls (who are drawn in love toward their guardians).

And the earthly beloved can play the role of the Angel. As Plato says in the *Phaedrus*,

> The newly initiated, who has had a full sight of the celestial vision, when he beholds a god-like face or a physical form which truly reflects ideal beauty, first of all shivers and experiences something of the dread which the vision itself inspired; next he gazes upon it and worships it as if were a god, and if he were not afraid of being thought an utter madman, he would sacrifice to his beloved as to the image of a divinity.

Daniel in the lion's den is protected by Guardian Angels. From a commentary on the *Apocalypse* by the Spanish monk Beatus de Liebana (d.798); now in the British Library, London

75

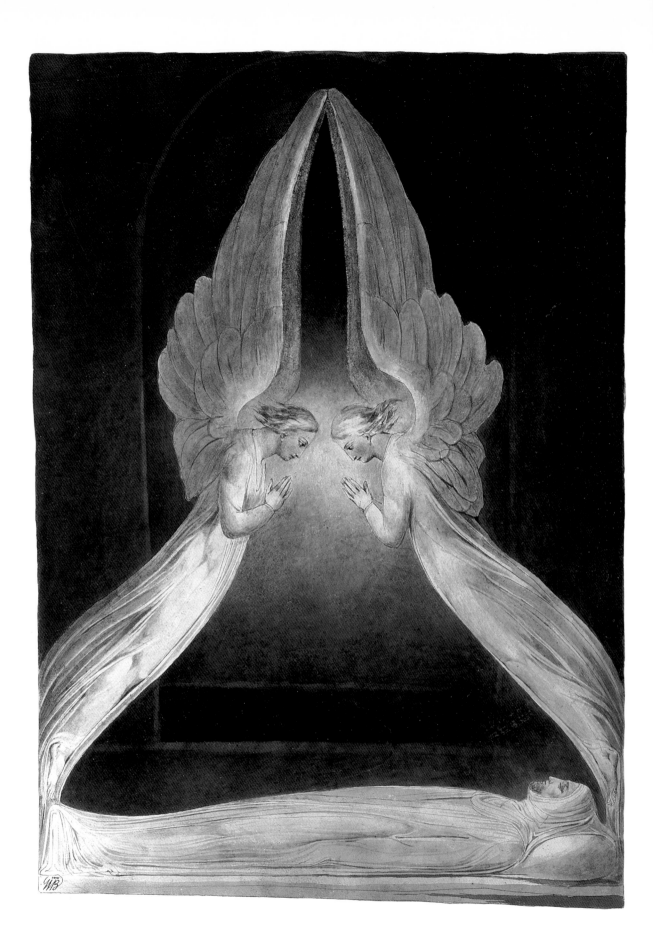

The ladder

And he dreamed, and behold a ladder set up on the earth, and the top of it reached to heaven: and behold, the Angels of God ascending and descending.   GENESIS 28

Jacob, after his dream of the Angelic Ladder, 'was afraid, and said, How dreadful is this place! This is none other but the house of God, and this is the gate of heaven.'

'As above, so below', says the *Emerald Tablet of Hermes Trismegistus*. And Jacob's Ladder tells us that the way down is the way up. St John Chrysostom invites us to think of 'that spiritual ladder which the Patriarch Jacob saw stretching from earth to heaven. The Angels were coming down along it and the martyrs were going up. You have often seen the sun rise in the morning, darting out purple-tinted rays in every direction. Such were the bodies of the martyrs: the crimson tide of their blood had flooded every part of them as with rays of purple and illuminated their bodies more than the sun lights up the heavens. The Angels gazed upon this blood with delight!'

The way of the mystic (who 'dies before death') is like the way of the martyr. Thus this ruby tint is the colour of the alchemic Stone, the crimson hue of Sophia or of the Archangel Gabriel.

The Ladder appears in every tradition. It is the tent-pole which the shaman climbs towards the smoke-hole of his hut: the Tree of Life. Mohammed's Ascent (*mir'aj*) is literally a ladder. In the Mithraic mysteries the initiate climbed a ladder (*klimax*) of seven rungs made of the seven planetary metals. In New Zealand, Indonesia, Melanesia, Japan and the southwest of the United States, the shaman climbs up a rainbow serpent whose seven colours represent the seven heavens. The Babylonian ziggurat was painted in these colours, and to climb it was to attain the summit of the cosmos. The Turk and Uighur shamans called their drums 'rainbow', and used them as magic mounts. Taoists in Taiwan and Yamabushi monks in Japan still perform the incredible feat of climbing in their bare feet a ladder built of razor-sharp swords, often as many as thirty-six.

St John climbing the ladder to Heaven; from a 13th-century manuscript in New College, Oxford.

Opposite: William Blake, *Angels Watching over the Tomb of Christ*, watercolour; c.1806; Victoria and Albert Museum, London

Orient and Hyperborea

Not every journey is a journey *to* the Angel, and not every way leads *up* in the strict sense of the word. Some seekers travel *with* the Angel, and *across* the face of an earth transformed by symbolic insight into a horizontal mirror image of the celestial or vertical ascent. The sacred direction then might be any one of the four: in Zoroastrianism the way leads South, in Celtic and American Indian lore West. Most Semitic writers favour the symbolism of the East, and in Aryan-influenced myth the direction is sometimes North. In all these cases the purpose is the same: as the sufis put it, to make a 'journey to the Outer Horizons' which will correspond to the 'journey to the Inner Horizons'. Thus one travels with the Angel, whose presence as guide permits one to find in the landscape the 'signs', the symbols, of true selfhood.

The Book of Tobit, one of the Old Testament Apocrypha, contains such an itinerary. Tobit is a pious Jew of good family, an exile in Nineveh. He suffers persecution from the gentiles, and through an accident he goes blind. He decides to send his young son Tobias to Persia to collect a debt from a business acquaintance there, and directs the boy to find some older person to accompany him. Tobias goes out looking, and meets a man he immediately likes and trusts. 'Canst thou go with me to Rages [Rayy, near modern Tehran]? and knowest thou those places well?' The man introduces himself to old Tobit as Azarias, a Jew of good reputation, and the journey is arranged. 'So they went forth both, and the young man's dog with them.'

In the evening they come to the banks of the Tigris. A fish leaps out of the water as if to seize Tobias, but Azarias shows him how to catch it. (Apparently it is meant to be a sort of water-dragon, though later artists depict it as a little trout.) The man directs the boy to cut out the fish's heart, liver and gall, which possess magic properties.

Now the scene shifts to Persia, where we learn of the strange plight of a young girl called Sara, daughter of Raguel (a cousin of Tobit's living in Ecbatana, near modern Hamadan). She is bewitched: she has been married to seven men, but all of them have been killed on their wedding night by the demon Asmodeus 'before they had lain with her'.

Soon the boy and his companion arrive in Ecbatana, and Azarias suggests that a marriage be arranged between Sara and Tobias. Naturally everyone is rather reluctant (especially Tobias), but Azarias instructs the youth to make an incense of the fish's heart and liver. On the wedding night he burns it; 'the which smell when the evil spirit had smelled, he fled into the utmost part of Egypt.'

Tobias and Sara spend the night in bliss, and next morning emerge unharmed to great rejoicing. While they enjoy a honeymoon Azarias goes to Ravy to collect the debt. The three of them (and the dog) then return to Nineveh. Azarias directs Tobias to make a salve of the fish's gall and anoint the blind eyes of Tobit, whereupon he recovers his sight. Tobit offers Azarias half his wealth in return for all this kindness, but the man refuses. He now reveals his true identity: 'I am Raphael, one of the seven holy Angels, which present the prayers of the saints, and which go in and out before the glory of the Holy One'. At first the mortals are afraid, but Raphael calms them, and with an order to write down all that has transpired, he vanishes. And they live happily ever after.

Tobias and the Angel, who accompanied him on his journey before revealing that he was Gabriel. Painting by Pollaiuolo in the Gallery at Turin.

Flights of Angels

The natural motion of Angels is upwards. Milton tells us that it requires an effort for them to go downwards. When human beings are taken up into heaven, it is the Angels who effortlessly lift them. There exist literally scores, perhaps hundreds, of accounts of heavenly ascensions. Obviously the symbolism, the archetype of the ascension, exercises a great fascination in every culture. In Christianity the Ascension of Christ and the Assumption of the Virgin are the best known, but similar stories occur in Islam (Mohammed's Night Journey) and in Near Eastern religious texts.

The idea of flying is associated with divinity even in the tribal customs of North American Indians, where the most powerful totemic animal is the eagle. The heraldry of the eagle is nearly universal, and so is man's desire to assimilate to himself eagle-like qualities of pride, courage and high-flying freedom. In most cultures the totemic bird is relegated to coins or flags, but there are Mexican bird dancers who recapture the very essence of being-an-eagle, of having wings and flying in trance, in dream, inside the self. In Japan, the Bagaku dancers follow a similar visionary path.

Child-like Angels carry the Virgin to heaven in a page from the Visconti Hours, 15th century. If angels are often depicted as children at play, it is because one way of looking at perfection is to see it as a 'Ludus puerorum', a child's game, with the endless purity and inventiveness of the untainted imagination.

Mohammed's famous Night Journey took him to heaven on the back of the Buraq, part Angel, part mule, accompanied by Gabriel and escorted by attendant angels (above, from a 16th-century Persian manuscript). The closest Christian analogy is Elijah, carried up to heaven on a fiery chariot: a Russian icon of the 16th century.

Overleaf:
On another Russian icon an Angel lifts a soul in ecstasy to heaven by the power of its upward motion. Right: in Persian mythology too Angels fly between earth and heaven as God directs them. This miniature is from Firdowsi's *Shahnameh*.

The forerunners of the cherubs and putti of Christian imagery are the little cupids, companions of Eros and Dionysus, of Roman art. In this mosaic from Tunisia they wage a mock war mounted on storks. Right: Japanese Bagaku dancers as Angels in a painting by Hanabusa Itchō (1652–1724). It is uncertain whether Japan borrowed the Angel figure from the ancient Middle East or vice-versa; but an archetype which is truly basic to human experience will appear simultaneously in all cultures.

The miraculous night journey

It is the one mighty in Power hath taught him, the Vigorous One; he grew clear to view as he hovered in the loftiest sphere; then he drew nigh and hovered in the air till he was distant two bows' lengths or nearer ... And verily he saw him yet another time by the lote-tree of the utmost boundary nigh unto which is the Garden of Abode. When that which shroudeth did enshroud the lote-tree, the eye turned not.

KORAN, LI, 5–17

According to the traditional interpretation of this text, Mohammed saw Gabriel in his cosmic form (as opposed to hearing him, or seeing him in the form of a man) only on the two occasions thus described. The vision of the lote-tree refers to the Prophet's *mir' aj* (his 'ladder' or Night Ascension). The Koran gives very few details, but the Prophet himself recounted more, and later folklore fleshed out the tale even further.

It takes place just after Mohammed has been chosen as a prophet. One night three Angels come to him while he sleeps, cut open his breast and tear out his heart. With water from the sacred well of Zam-Zam in Mecca, they wash the heart and lave away all that they find within him of doubt, idolatry, paganism and error. Then they fill the cavity with a liquid of wisdom poured from a golden vessel, replace the heart and sew up the breast again.

On the next night, 'I lay asleep in my house. It was a night in which there were thunder and lightning. No living beings could be heard, no bird journeyed. No one was awake, whereas I was not asleep; I dwelt between waking and sleeping.'

> Suddenly Gabriel the Archangel descended in his own form, of such beauty, of such sacred glory, of such majesty, that all my dwelling was illuminated. He is of a whiteness brighter than snow, his face is gloriously beautiful, the waves of his hair fall in long tresses, his brow is encircled as with a diadem of light on which is written 'There is no god but God'. He has six hundred wings set with 70,000 grains of red chrysolite.
>
> When he had approached me, he took me in his arms, kissed me between the eyes and said, 'O sleeper, how long wilt thou sleep? Arise! Tenderly will I guide thee. Fear not, for I am Gabriel thy brother.'

The Angel offers Mohammed a choice of three cups: one of wine, one of honey, one of milk. The Prophet starts to take the wine, but Gabriel corrects him and gives him the milk. According to the commentators, wine is the animal 'breath', honey the physical 'breath' and milk the mental 'breath'.

Gabriel now brings Mohammed a supernatural mount, the Buraq, a winged mule with a woman's face. The Buraq (like Garuda) represents the contemplative mind – it is restive, and the Angel must calm it before Mohammed can ride.

They soar into the sky, hover for an instant over the Kaaba, and whirl away towards the north. In an instant they have arrived in Jerusalem at the Farthest Mosque, the Dome of the Rock. Here the muezzin is giving the call to prayer. They enter and find an assembly of Angels and prophets, who welcome them.

Opposite:
Angels gaze down from the ceiling of the church of Debre Berhan in Ethiopia. All reality is one, but to the seeker who has not yet reached perfection, it seems to unfold as a system of ascending levels of reality like the rungs of a ladder: carnal, mental, psychic, spiritual – and finally, total union with the Principle beyond all becoming. At each such stage there is an Angel to be encountered: guardian of the threshold, but also the very substance of the experience within.

In the Eighteenth Canto of the
Paradiso, Dante describes the
Primùm Mobile and the Nine
Orders of Angels. In this drawing
by Botticelli, Dante and his guide
Beatrice stand in the foreground;
the circles of Angels, each one
differentiated, surround them,
and at the top, lightly sketched,
is the Trinity.

Beatrice explains it to him; then as she falls silent, he sees innumerable Angels:

> *thick as the sparks from molten iron sped*
> *so did the sparks about the circles chase . . . .*
> *From choir to choir I heard Hosanna rolled*
> *to that fixt point which holds them in their home,*
> *hath held them ever, and shall forever hold.*

Beatrice tells him that the highest choirs derive their bliss from *seeing* God:

> *. . . the celestial bliss*
> *is founded on the act that seeth God,*
> *not that which loves, which cometh after this.*

In other words, gnosis or knowledge is higher than Love.

Beatrice points out each of the Orders in descending rank, and comments:

> *Upwards these Orders gaze; and so prevails*
> *downward their power, that up toward God on high*
> *all are impelled, and each in turn impels;*

thus interpreting Dionysius's teachings on the initiation of the Angels.

She now goes on to comment in a special way on the Areopagite's teachings on the Creation:

> *Not increase of His own good to proclaim*
> *(which is not possible) but that His own*
> *splendour might in resplendence say I Am;*
> *In His eternity, where time is none,*
> *nor aught of limitation else, He chose*
> *that in new loves the eternal Love be shown.*

In Mohammed's words: 'God was a hidden treasure, and He desired or "loved" to be known; so He created the world that He might be known.'

The Angels have from the beginning kept their vision fixed on God's face. Each Angel is a separate species, since each possesses its own mode of absorbing and reflecting the primal light which irradiates it:

> *And since on the mind's vision love ensues,*
> *that sweetness glows within them fiery-bright*
> *or warm, according to the mode they use.*
> *See now the Eternal Virtue's breadth and height,*
> *since it hath made itself so vast a store*
> *of mirrors upon which to break its light,*
> *Remaining in itself one, as before.*